TUXEDO
BABY

PERU

CHILE

by Victoria Smith

illustrated by Helen Stebakov

ISBN 978-1-7378135-0-7 Paperback
ISBN 978-1-7378135-1-4 E-book
ISBN 978-1-7378135-2-1 Hard Copy

Library of Congress Control Number
2021918113

Dedication

To my family, who knew about Tuxedo Baby a long time ago and encouraged me to write.

To my editor, Katie Chambers, who guided me with the words I used and made my book better.

To my illustrator, Helen Stebakov, who gave life to Tuxedo Baby.

Lastly, to Self-Publishing School, who worked with me step by step in the process of writing and helping my book come to fruition.

A long time ago, an oil spill left Tuxedo Baby, a penguin, alone. Although he was cared for by his colony, they couldn't offer him what he wanted the most: two loving parents.

Luckily, a Mr. and Mrs. Conure, cherry-headed parrots, heard about the orphaned penguin through the whispers of the wind. They wanted a baby, so they flew from Peru to Chile to pick up Tuxedo Baby and raise him as their own.

Tuxedo Baby wanted to belong and learn.

Although the Conures taught him how to make his bed,

play with toys,

and even screech loudly, at over 120 decibels, as conures do,

Tuxedo Baby wanted more than ever to be just like them and fly.

After several months, Tuxedo Baby was old enough to go to school. This wasn't a school where he'd learn how to fish and survive, like other penguins. No, this school taught the students how to hunt and soar.

Tuxedo Baby loved watching his friends spread their wings and take off. He only dreamed that one day he could fly like them.

Louie, his friend from bird school, had an idea!
"Hey, Tuxedo Baby, I know how to help you fly," he said.
"What? Really? Show me," said Tuxedo Baby.
So, Louie came over after school, and together
they came up with the perfect plan.

Tuxedo Baby wore a Halloween costume with angel wings. Louie said, "Stand on the tallest furniture in the house that you can reach."

"Okay, how about that?" said Tuxedo Baby.

Tuxedo Baby was standing on his mother's bedroom dresser. Louie counted, "One, two, three." On three, Tuxedo Baby jumped with his eyes closed.

Unfortunately, gravity pulled him smashing
down. The fall broke his mom's perfectly
arranged glass ornaments on the table below,
and he got really banged up. Landing on his face,
he broke the flesh spines on the inside of his mouth.
Tuxedo Baby screeched for his mom.

Mrs. Conure came flying in upon hearing the commotion from her bedroom. Louie flew home quickly, and Mrs. Conure bandaged Tuxedo Baby up.

Then she picked up the broken pieces from her collection of glass ornaments. Lovingly, she held Tuxedo Baby, saying, "Honey, you are a penguin.

Penguins can't fly!"

The following week, Tuxedo Baby wanted to have a friend over to play ball. Although Mrs. Conure was okay with another friend visiting, she reminded him what happened last time.

"I know, Mom. We are just playing ball," said Tuxedo Baby.

On Wednesday, after bird school, Huey came over. They were having a fun time laughing, eating, and playing. "Look, look, I can hit the ball with my flippers," said Tuxedo Baby. Tuxedo Baby was hitting the ball pretty well, using his flippers, until they both saw the ball . . .

go past the grass,

fly past the patio,

skid off the garage...

...and crash into the kitchen window. "No, I'm in so much trouble. Fly home, Huey, before my mom comes flying out!" screeched Tuxedo Baby. Huey flew so fast he almost ran into Mr. Conure coming home. "Hey, Huey, what's the rush?" he said. Instantly, Mr. Conure knew why Huey had flown out of there so fast. Mrs. Conure was fuming and screeching loudly. Tuxedo Baby hung his head and peeked up at his parents. They looked mad. He said, "Sorry I disappointed you."

Lovingly, they told him they admired his willingness to try things, but they also didn't like all the things getting broken lately.

Mrs. Conure said, "You are a penguin, not a conure, so you need to be aware of your limitations. But you are capable of greatness, and I love that you want to try new things. Please continue to do so, but know your limitations and be careful."

The Conures wanted to share good news to cheer them all up, especially after today. They had the perfect news, but they weren't sure if Tuxedo Baby was ready. But then they realized he was growing up, getting bigger and stronger. He was now over fourteen inches tall and about six pounds.

Mrs. Conure said, "Tuxedo Baby, you are growing up, and we have some good news for you. You are going to be a big brother."

"Whaaat?" he said.

The Conures told him he would have a baby sister in twenty-five days.

Anxious to see how Tuxedo Baby felt about this, since he had been an only child, they carefully watched Tuxedo Baby for his reaction.

But, to their relief, Tuxedo
Baby was jumping up and down.
He couldn't contain his excitement.
"I will have a new baby to teach. I can show her how to
waddle. I will teach her how to screech at over 120
decibels. I will teach my baby sister how to cuddle and
love," said Tuxedo Baby proudly.

Tuxedo Baby and the Conures held each other tightly. They were so happy to share the good news with Tuxedo Baby. Mr. and Mrs. Conure promised Tuxedo Baby that after his sister had settled in, they would invite the Magellanic Penguin Colony, migrating in winter to Peru, to drop in and visit with him and his family.

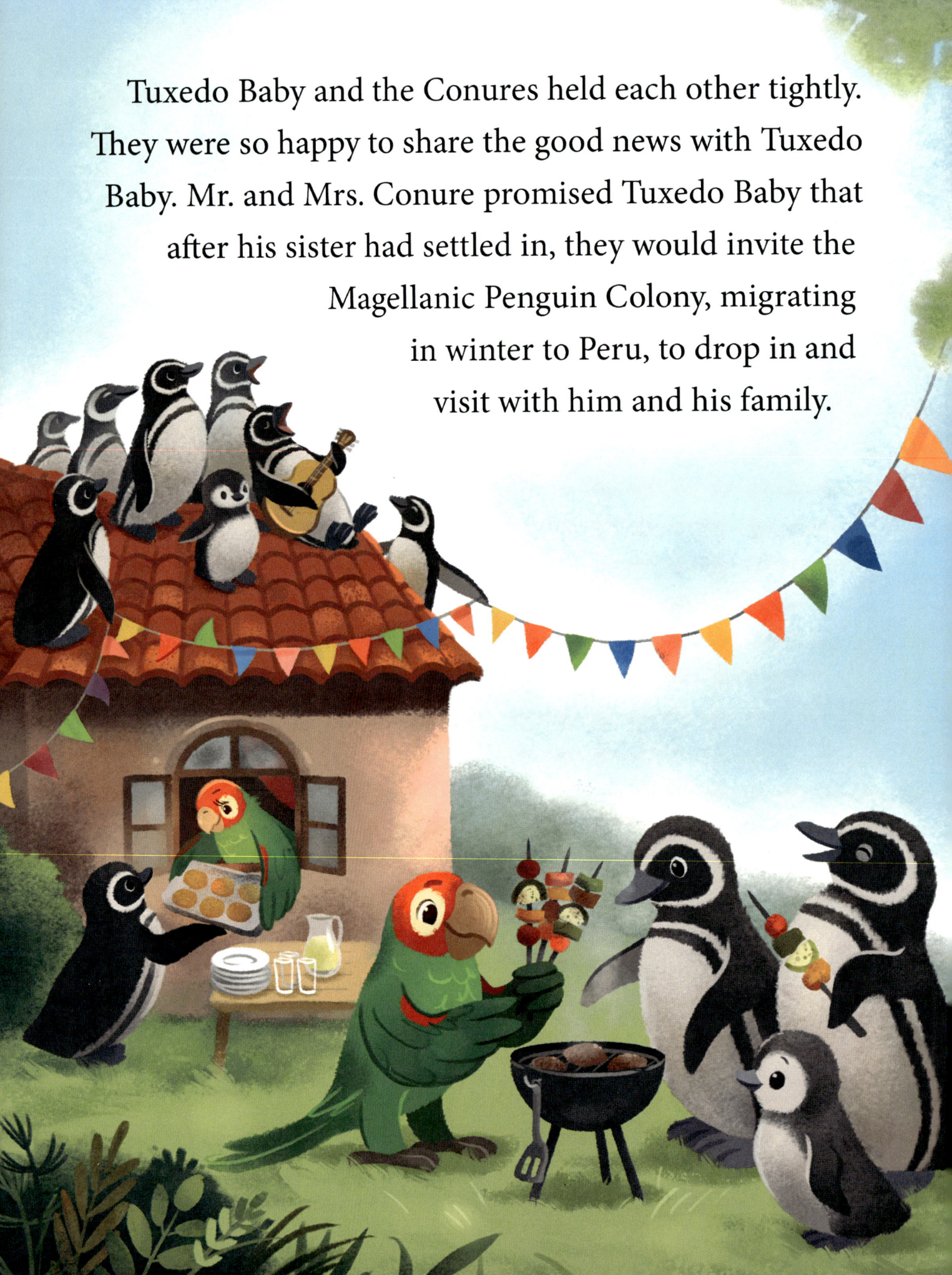

Life was great. The future was bright. Tuxedo Baby knew he was fortunate to have the Conures, a new baby sister on the way, and the excitement of having his penguin family come to visit.

Smiling, Tuxedo Baby looked at his parents and said, "Well, I can't be Tuxedo Baby forever, and I'm getting bigger, so maybe you can call me Tux, big brother, from now on." The Conures smiled, cuddled, and loved him so much.

Facts about Cherry-Head Conures:

Cherry-Head Conures, also called Red Masked or Christmas Conures, are related to the Macaws; have green bodies, red around the head and on the wings, and a white ring around their eyes; and, at thirteen inches long, are a medium-sized bird. The beak is horn-colored, and they have gray feet. They can live for about twenty-five years, and some can live up to fifty years.

If you train them, a few can talk. In the recent past, due to their piercing screeches, many owners have let these birds go freely. Their shriek sound can be deafening. While they come from Peru and Ecuador, they have about four hundred of these birds in San Francisco.

In the wild, they eat nuts, seeds, fruit, and vegetables. They love to bathe by opening their wings to catch raindrops, which keeps their plumage healthy and beautiful.

These birds can have a lot of character. Some like to bob their heads to music. Others can cuddle and be affectionate. Some can scream and bite. Owning a bird like this requires patience and a lot of love for this animal who will make you part of its flock.[1]

---

1. Tony Silva and Barbara Kotlar, Conures (New Jersey: TFH Publications, Inc., 1989).

Facts about Magellanic Penguins:

Magellanic Penguins live in South America. They can be twenty-four to thirty inches tall and weigh six to fourteen pounds. Their black back and white abdomen protects them from prey while swimming in the ocean.

These penguins also can be found at the San Francisco Zoo in California. They can live up to twenty-five years in the wild and thirty in captivity.

When hunting for food, plankton, squid, and small fish, they travel in large flocks.

They make a trumpeting type of call or screeching sound. Their mating call helps them find partners, which they bond with for life. From September to late February, they breed. Chicks are cared for by both parents. Once the breeding season is over, Magellanic Penguins migrate north for winter, where they feed in waters offshore from Peru and Brazil.[2]

---

2. Penguins: An Educational Coloring Book (Rapid City, SD: Spizzirri Publishing Company, 1989). Illustrated by Peter M. Spizzirri; "Magellanic Penguins," last modified September 9, 2021, https://en.wikipedia.org/wiki/Magellanic_penguin.

Facts about Oil Spills:

It has been estimated that over 40,000 Magellanic Penguins have been killed each year by chronic oil pollution along the coast of Chubut Province, Argentina, from 1982–1991.

Oil spills are caused by accidents, people, or broken equipment. These accidents could be crude oil from tankers, drilling, rigs, or spills of petroleum products, like gasoline or diesel fuel. While some causes are natural disasters, others are deliberate acts. Whatever the cause, all oil spills have environmental and economic effects. Oil spills caused by petroleum pollution are the main cause for death among adult penguins.

Penguins have special feathers that protect them from the cold waters they swim in. When these feathers are soaked in oil in the ocean, it increases their risk of hypothermia (drop in body temperature).[3]

_____

3. Pablo Garcia-Borboroglu, P. Dee Boserma, Laura Marina Reyes, et.al. "Petroliam Pollution and Penguins: Marine Conservation Tools to Reduce the Problem," in Marine Pollution: New Research, ed. Tobias N. Hofer (New York: Nova Science Publishers), 339–356, https://oilspill.fsu.edu/images/pdfs/oil-pollution-penguins.pdf; "Oil spill," last modified September 12, 2021, https://en.wikipedia.org/wiki/Oil_spill; "Oil Spills," MedlinePlus, US

About the author

Victoria is a retired teacher with a Masters in Reading who now enjoys writing children's books. She lives in Alameda, Ca. with her pet dog, Daisy, her 3-legged cat, Smokey, and her box turtle, Swimmy.

Victoria loves animals. She has always surrounded herself with them at home and in the classroom.

welovebooks@familyzooproductions.com